THE
CAT
YEAR

CATS, MAGIC, NATURE AND SPELLS

ALISON DAVIES

Illustrated by
Anastasia Stefurak

quadrille

CONTENTS

Introduction 6

WELCOME

The enigma of the feline is a timeless conundrum, and something which continues to fascinate humankind. Try as we might to put them in a box, metaphorically speaking (though they'd prefer one made out of cardboard), to categorize a cat is an impossible feat. They cannot be defined by the usual rules because they do not conform to what is expected. Cats go their own way and they do it with a panache that is all puss. Their sanguine, ready-for-anything cattitude is something we humans cannot help but admire. It's no wonder they have captured our hearts and minds for centuries.

We cannot fathom what makes the feline tick, and so we imagine, in the hopes that we'll make sense of the mystery. We give them mythical status and powers, which are not far from the truth when you consider the many gifts they have at their disposal. We believe we can understand them, and to a degree, we can learn by reading body language and the various signs they give us to communicate their needs. But it will always be on their terms. These magnificent animals do not need our approval. If anything, it is us as humans that seek feline appreciation and understanding. We want them to like us because they are different, quirky and ethereal.

It is not a huge stretch of the imagination to believe that fairies once held court within their eyes, and that if you were to stare for long enough, you might catch a glimpse of the fey otherworld. Equally, we can almost accept the link between cats and witches, and the belief that one could transform into the other, or that felines were once worshipped as deities and had the ability to bestow good fortune. It might be just folklore, but there is always a kernel of truth to the tale, an underlying belief that there is more than meets the eye when it comes to the moggy.

If you're a proud puss parent, you will understand this truth, for you will see evidence of it day-to-day. From the way your cat moves and grooves, to the things it does that surprise you, cats have a habit of doing the unexpected, and they do it exceedingly well. Like us, they go through changes in life, some with the onset of time, and others with the shift in the seasons. They react to their environment and work with it (felines have always been able to make the most of any situation), choosing to domesticate themselves by catching mice and rats in the grain stores, then cozying up to the ever-so-grateful humans at night.

This book is a celebration of all things cat. It goes some way to examining their mystery and provides a glimmer of insight into the feline realm, with seasonal introductions that chart the changes every cat will experience throughout the year, and sections on myth, folklore and superstition. Each month, a different breed is showcased, and new stories are shared along with fascinating facts and things to look out for when trying to build a relationship with your cat. There's a section on cat chat that aims to reveal what your kitty might be saying, and some suggestions for feline fun. There's also a cat-inspired spell to help you tap into their magic and form a psychic bond with them, and some kitty-influenced yoga moves and stretches.

Month by month, you will delve into the mystical world of the moggy, and form a deeper understanding of their true nature. But remember, what is offered here is simply a starting point from which to explore – a delightful and enchanting piece of the puzzle. Cats are not meant to be fully deciphered. Loved, respected and talked about, most definitely, but always with an air of mystery and a degree of admiration that is befitting for the fabulous feline. Welcome to *The Cat Year*, the purrfect way to celebrate these amazing creatures!

JANUARY

CAT OF THE MONTH

NORWEGIAN FOREST

This striking feline was so favoured by King Olaf V of Norway that he made it the country's national treasure. Magnificent in stature and might, but surprisingly playful (despite their warrior roots) because they take longer than most other cats to mature to adulthood. While the breed's true origins remain a mystery, scholars surmise that this breed is the descendant of a long-haired kitty from Scandinavia, carried to foreign shores by the crusaders.

Originally found wandering the mountainous landscape and interbreeding with other feral species, these cats, also known as Wedgies, are larger than most other species of house cat. But don't let size put you off. These super-furry giants make for friendly companions with kitten-like tendencies. With a dense coat made up of a woolly underside and an outer layer of longer, waterproof fur, this is a puss built to survive and thrive during the winter months.

CAT SUPERSTITION

THE CAT'S SNEEZE

The mystical reputation of the cat is as long as its tail, and just as baffling. The humble sneeze might just suggest your cat has been sticking its delicate nose into a dusty crevice, but it could also be a fortuitous omen. It is said that hearing a cat sneeze at close range means good fortune is on its way, and an unexpected windfall could land in your lap.

In Italy, if a bride hears a cat sneeze on their wedding day, then the marriage will be a good one, and if that cat is black, then they are doubly blessed. If you want to know who will be next up the aisle, then take note of who the cat looks at after washing its face, for they will soon wed. And for the health-conscious, watch out if you hear a cat sneeze three times or more – someone you know will be struck down with a cold!

THE CAT'S WHISKERS

CAT'S EYES

There's no denying the power of your cat's stare. Those captivating peepers pull you in, and within seconds you are lost in a lingering gaze. Despite their lack of eyelashes, cats keep their eyes in tip-top condition with an extra eyelid known as a haw, which protects their eyes from debris and infection. The *palpebra tertia*, or nictating membrane, as it is also called, is only slightly visible when they're fully alert and on the prowl. But its presence is important. It acts like a windshield wiper and protects the cornea from injury. No wonder their eyes glisten with such promise!

FELINE MYTH

THE SKOGKATT

Step into the woods on a misty morn before sunrise, when the icy air chills you to the bone, and you might cross paths with the infamous Skogkatt, a piece of old Norse magic. While this humungous creature prowls in the shadows, there is little to fear here. The Skogkatt, meaning forest cat, is blessed with fairy charm, and certainly wouldn't harm a hapless wanderer.

Renowned for its supernatural strength, the Skogkatt was revered by the gods and goddesses, and was even thought to be a match for their brute force. According to legend, Thor, the god of thunder, faced the World Serpent Jörmungandr in a challenge of strength. While Thor was thought to be one of the most powerful deities in the Norse pantheon, Jörmungandr was clever and transformed into a colossal Skogkatt, making it impossible for the god to defeat him.

As enchanting as they are enormous, these mystical felines always have the upper paw, whether they're scaling the treetops or standing their ground in a magical face off. They are Goliath in spirit and attitude.

CAT STRETCH

THE WAIST WHITTLER

Cats know it is essential to encourage blood flow in the morning with a few lazy but effective stretches. But nothing too taxing; the emphasis is on relaxing into the day and firing up those core muscles. Whether you've got the January blues or you just want to pull some moves, this month's stretch will help you face the day or month with cattitude.

· Lie on your back, take a long slow breath in and bring your knees gently up towards your chest. You might want to hold them there for a few seconds by wrapping your arms around them.

- Keep your legs bent and together, and when you're ready, stretch your arms out to the sides.

- As you release your breath, slowly twist from your waist, letting your knees fall to one side.

- Hold this position for thirty seconds, then take another deep breath in, and pull in your core. Bring your legs back to the centre using your tummy muscles.

- Repeat on the other side.

CAT CHAT

HEADS OR TAILS?

From headbutts to bottom struts, your cat tells you exactly how it's feeling using every part of its carefully constructed anatomy. A gentle headbutt is your kitty's way of saying, 'Hello, you lovely human.' It's an affectionate gesture, which means, 'You're OK, I like you.'

A forceful and repetitive head pump is your cat's way of knocking on the door. Like an insistent, 'I'm here!', it announces their arrival, and suggests you drop everything immediately to pay them some attention.

Should you be on the receiving end of a bottom butt to the face, do not despair; this too is a mark of how much they trust you. When they present their perfectly poised derrière for your inspection, they are saying, 'This is me. This is where I've been and what I smell like. Enjoy!'

FELINE UPCYCLING

You don't need to invest in the latest toys and gadgets to keep your kitty occupied. Sometimes the most surprising things provide hours of entertainment, from a smelly old sock to a scrunched-up piece of foil. As long as it's light, bright and easy to chase and retrieve safely, it can be used in an interactive game. What's more, it's a brilliant way to recycle magazines and papers, or bits of cloth.

If you're feeling crafty and creative, why not stuff an old sock with a handful of dried catnip or valerian? These herbs are the feline dream team, inspiring fun and frolics and helping to keep your cat chilled. Sew up the end of the sock and leave it in their favourite spot to help them get used to their new toy.

CAT SPELL

SPELL TO STOP YOUR CAT FROM ROAMING

Cats are the great adventurers of the animal kingdom. They love to wander and forage. To them, the outdoors is a giant playground packed with deliciously tempting sights, sounds and smells. If your furry friend tends to roam too far and get into mischief, this simple spell will draw them closer to home.

You will need: an old collar belonging to your cat, a black velvet charm bag or black scarf, catnip, pinch of sea salt

Perform this spell on a Friday evening. Friday is associated with the Norse goddess Freya, who kept her cat companions close upon her travels.

- Take the collar and hold it in both hands.
- Close your eyes and picture your cat.
- Spend a few minutes thinking about how much you love spending time with them and what they mean to you.
- Take a deep breath in and as you exhale, say, 'Wander if you must my little puss, but never too far from me would you want to be.'
- Place the collar into the bag or in the centre of the scarf.
- Add a pinch of catnip to the bundle to attract your feline and boost positive energy, and finish by sprinkling a little salt into the bag or scarf for protection.
- Tie the bag, or bundle up the scarf and tie it loosely, then keep it somewhere safe near where you sleep.

FEBRUARY

CAT OF THE MONTH

RAGDOLL

This semi long-haired beauty is a bundle of love wrapped in the prettiest furry packaging. While they may be large and muscular, the regal ruff around the neck signals a noble, gentle breed that loves to spend time with its family. As the Ragdoll name suggests, they're a cuddly and sometimes floppy feline – but they are not playthings and should be treated with respect and adoration.

Baby Ragdolls come into the world pure white in hue, and only develop their distinctive shaded pattern after a few weeks. All cats within the breed have dazzling blue eyes, which can vary in shade depending on their mix of ancestry. Like dogs, Ragdolls are incredible loyal and trusting, and have been even known to enjoy a game of fetch.

FAIRY CATS AND COURTS

The Celts believed in the mystical power of cats, and even thought they were fairies in animal form. Like other fey beings, fairy cats had courts that gathered together, and were ruled by a king or queen. It was their responsibility to guard the kingdom and protect any treasure from magical looters. Humans, being so entranced by the feline form, would stare into their cats' eyes, believing they might catch a glimpse of this magical otherworld, and, if they were really lucky, see the king or queen gazing back at them.

According to legend, these magical moggies lived as house sprites amongst their people, but should time command it, would leave their post to return to the fairy otherworld at the twitch of a whisker. One popular Celtic tale tells of a man who learns that his beloved feline is the next King of the Cats, called to arms after the death of his predecessor. This early folk story from the British Isles has a number of variations. In some tales, house cats were fairies who had been banished from their kingdom, so they made the choice to shift shape and live in the human world instead.

CAT SUPERSTITION

THE COLOUR OF CATS

In India, grey cats are auspicious and, should one cross your path, you can expect to be blessed with good fortune. The same can be said if you meet three black cats together; all of your endeavours will be well starred. If you set out upon a journey or new venture and you spy a cat upon your left side, this too is an omen signifying that all will go well, and you will be prosperous in whatever you do. Cats of any shape, size or colour are thought to be symbols of fertility in the Hindu faith, and if your house is blessed with the pitter patter of kitten feet thanks to your feline giving birth, then expect a windfall or some other monetary gain. That said, if you hear a cat caterwauling when leaving your home, be warned – there may be trouble ahead.

THE CAT'S WHISKERS

FELINE GOOD

Cats heal their humans in a number of ways. Stroking a kitty not only lowers blood pressure, but it also releases the feel-good hormone oxytocin, which calms and balances the emotions. This helps to keep low moods at bay and gives cat parents a much-needed boost. Then there's the low, rumbling purr, like melted chocolate. It's a sound many owners know and enjoy, and it's a cat's secret weapon. The magic occurs when the purr falls between 25 and 150 hertz. At this level it aids the healing of bones by improving their density, and also mends other wounds. It's no surprise that the soothing sound lowers the heart rate too – and the good news is that cats *also* feel the benefit.

CAT CHAT

A HAIR AND A WHISKER

A cat's whiskers are more than just a pretty addition to their face. Their whiskers act like antennae, helping the cat feel its way around in the dark. Attached to the muscles and the nervous system, these spiny tendrils send messages to the brain, which aid navigation. They can also detect changes in the air and help to provide spatial awareness.

Even more impressively, the perfectly coiffured filaments of hair reveal how your feline feels at any given time. When they hang low and loose towards the ground, your cat is relaxed and ready for downtime. But if you notice the whiskers pointing forwards or slightly up, know that kitty is primed and ready to pounce. If the whiskers are slightly pulled back, then your feline is fearful, and feeling threatened in some way.

CAT STRETCH

THE ON-ALL-FOURS STRETCH

This gentle stretch brings you close to the ground, providing stability while helping to centre your balance. It's a stretch that your cat has perfected and performs just before it gets comfortable for a nap. This is the perfect move to practise when you're feeling stressed, or you simply need some time out.

- Start by getting on all fours, with your knees and forearms on the floor.
- Take a deep breath in and bring your forehead down to rest on the floor too.
- Hold the breath to the count of four slow beats, then exhale slowly.
- As you do this, let your weight fall back onto your legs and raise your head. Your upper arms will naturally lift from the floor and stretch out in front of you.
- Hold your breath to the count of four long beats.

TRAIN YOUR CAT

Cats are clever; they enjoy a challenge and need stimulation, particularly if they spend a lot of time indoors. They respond well to training, especially when rewarded with their favourite treat.

Start with a simple game that encourages your cat to respond to its name. Let them see and sniff the treat in your hand, then move away and call their name. When they come towards you, present them with the treat as a reward. Repeat the process several times so that this behaviour sticks, then try something a little more challenging, like a high five paw-to-hand manoeuvre. Keep the treat in your raised hand and encourage them to tap with their paw, then let them have their reward.

CAT SPELL

SPELL TO STRENGTHEN THE BOND OF LOVE BETWEEN YOU AND YOUR CAT

Love and trust go paw-in-hand and help to make your puss feel safe and secure. It can take time with some cats, particularly if they've had a bad start in life, but there are magical rituals that you can perform to strengthen the ties between you and your cat.

You will need: a pin, a pink candle, a lighter or matches, a cozy blanket, a polished piece of rose quartz

Perform this spell when the moon is waxing (getting bigger). You can do this any evening in this moon phase, and it's a ritual that you can repeat several times over the course of a month. It helps if you can perform this spell when your cat is present.

· Take the pin and carve your cat's name into the candle wax. The pink candle promotes loving energy.

· Light the candle and gaze into the flame. Breathe slowly and deeply and let the flickering light soothe you. The flame ignites and strengthens the bonds between you.

· Wrap the blanket around your shoulders and hold the rose quartz in both hands. This beautiful, gentle stone boosts the flow of love between you and your cat.

· Continue to breathe deeply and as you exhale, imagine all the love you feel being absorbed by the blanket.

· Let the candle burn down, and place the blanket on your cat's bed, or favourite place to chill.

· Keep the rose quartz with you to open your heart and increase those loving vibes.

SPRING

As the earth warms beneath the paws and spring arrives
in a flurry of buds and midsummer dew, so a gentle
transformation takes place. The wheel of the year is
turning, and the light of the sun, which seemed so scarce
in the winter months, floods the landscape. The earlier
mornings bring a brightness that tickles the whiskers and
puts some pounce in the feline flounce. Our cats feel the
changes just as keenly as we do, and their moods will
match the joy of the season, as they wake earlier to greet
the day. There's no time for breakfast in bed when your
kitty has a hefty dose of spring fever.

With vitality restored, the listless haze of the darker
months lifts, and this means more energy for play and to
explore the great outdoors. You might also notice a shift
in their appearance as they shed their thicker insulating
fur. They'll probably be feline frisky too, thanks to a boost
in hormones. With all this extra energy to burn, don't be
surprised if they don a new slimline shape, and lose a
bit of belly girth. It's all part of the fun that comes with a
seasonal reboot.

MARCH

CAT OF THE MONTH

SIAMESE

One of the oldest breeds in the world, the Siamese hails from Thailand – formerly the ancient land of Siam – and is an enigma wrapped in fur. Sleek yet regal in appearance, with almond-shaped eyes and lithe limbs, it's no wonder these kitties were revered. It's thought that only those of royal blood or noble persuasion were allowed to home such cats. A spiritual companion in life and death, it is said that when a member of the family passed away, the spirit would seek refuge in this beloved feline. The kitty would then be pampered and worshipped within the temple until the end of its days. It was common belief that by treating the cat with honour, you blessed the soul it housed and eased its journey onto the next life.

Intelligent, highly affectionate and strikingly beautiful, the Siamese has feline film-star looks and a gregarious personality. This chatty cat enjoys being vocal throughout the day and has been known to demand attention by mimicking the cries of a baby.

CAT SUPERSTITION

FORTUITOUS FELINES

Cats and abundance are said to go paw-in-hand throughout the world. Synonymous with prosperity, the fortuitous feline has the power to bestow all manner of worldly riches upon its owner. Even those visiting a home with a cat will be blessed, according to one English tradition, which suggests kissing the cat of the house will attract a sudden windfall. Russians prize kitties with blue eyes, and believe that if one crosses your path, you'll receive good fortune, while in Japan, the Bobtail is a particularly auspicious sign and revered above all other felines. Older cats are considered luckier than younger ones in China, and it's thought that lighter-coated cats bring silver to their owners, while those with darker fur attract gold.

FELINE MYTH

THE LUCKY CAT

The lucky cat, or the beckoning cat, originates from Japanese folklore. Known in Japanese as the maneki neko, this friendly white cat, with pert red ears and a jaunty wave, is an iconic symbol of good fortune, and a representation of Tama, the pet of the abbot of the Gōtoku-ji temple in Setagaya. According to legend, the daimyo – the regional ruler during the Edo period – was out hunting when a terrible storm hit. The lightning bolts destroyed everything in their path. Luckily Tama was on hand and, raising a distinctive paw, he beckoned the daimyo into the temple and saved his life. From that day forwards the little cat, thought to be a Japanese Bobtail, was made a patron of the temple with a shrine in its honour.

This tradition has been carried through the ages, and the maneki neko is a popular sight, particularly in businesses that cite the figurine's power to increase prosperity and bring custom through the door. As a symbol, this cat represents the close relationship that Japanese people have always had with their felines, and their belief that if they care for a cat, the cat will take care of them, chasing away vermin and bringing bountiful blessings to their door.

FELINE FUN

HIDE AND SEEK

Cats enjoy the thrill of the chase, and they're natural hunters, so tap into these instincts by playing a game of hide and seek. Make things interesting by involving their favourite foodie treats. To begin, call your kitty and make it known that you have a handful of biscuits. Then run to another room and hide. When they find you, reward them with a treat and while they're munching, run and hide in a different room. Do this throughout house, and create a cat treat trail, or scatter single biscuits like breadcrumbs to lead them to you. This simple game can help your cat be more active, and it's great for fussy eaters who will be encouraged by the playful aspect of the challenge.

THE CAT'S WHISKERS

THE NOSE KNOWS

Cute as a button, a cat's nose sits neatly in the middle of its face. But this tiny pink jewel is more than a decorative accessory. The nose hides over 200 million sensors, which allows a cat to identify and track the subtlest of scents, as opposed to humans, who only have around 5 million sensors. With a sense of smell that's forty times more powerful than anything we could imagine, a cat's nose knows what's for tea before you've reached for the tin opener. A cat's sniffer is also as unique as a human fingerprint. With a variety of tiny bumps and ridges which can be seen when magnified, each nose is different – and can reveal who stole the salmon in a single twitch.

CAT STRETCH

THE SUPERMAN ROLL

This playful stretch is all about promoting a sense of fun and spontaneity. Based on a move that cats do freely and often just because it feels good, this manoeuvre will help you relax and fire up your senses.

· Lie on the floor on your tummy. Let your forehead rest on the back of your hands, keeping your arms bent.

· Close your eyes and take a deep breath in. As you do, notice how the floor feels beneath your body.

· As you release the breath, extend your arms out in front of you and stretch your legs. Point your toes and fingers as if replicating the Superman pose.

· Take another long breath and rock from side to side until you roll over completely.

· As you do this, release the breath and engage all your senses. Notice what you feel, see, hear, taste and smell.

· Relax and enjoy lying on your back, supported by the ground.

CAT CHAT

PUSS POSTURE

A cat's body shape and the way it holds itself reveals much about its mood. A relaxed, happy cat has a normal stance and will usually face you head on if it's confident in your company. A side-on approach suggests some shyness; the cat is pointing its body in a direction to provide an easy escape, should it need it. An anxious and fearful feline will crouch down into a ball, making itself small while protecting its internal organs, but a puffed-up kitty with an arched back is feeling angry and may even be aggressive. If a cat lies on its back with its belly exposed, it's a sign that it trusts you, but be warned, this does not mean a belly rub is on the cards. Look for other clues, like friendly miaows and purring before taking the plunge.

CAT SPELL

SPELL TO HELP CATS IN A MULTI-CAT HOUSEHOLD GET ALONG

Cats, like humans, have different personalities, and they are also naturally solitary creatures. They can get along purrfectly, but like any family you may also experience issues, and a few disagreements. Try this spell to help your fur family bond.

You will need: a piece of ginger to represent each cat (of roughly the same size and shape), some twine or wool, a velvet charm bag, fresh lavender flowers

Perform this spell when the moon is waxing, to help 'grow' the bond between your felines.

· Take the pieces of ginger and wrap the twine or wool around them to bind them, then tie in a knot to secure. As you do this, say, 'Together bound to get along, with give and take, no right or wrong. In harmony, you two/three/ four shall gel, from this moment on, all is well.'

· Put the pieces in the charm bag with a few lavender flowers which promote peace, then put it somewhere safe, preferably near a fire or hearth, which is considered to be the centre of the home.

APRIL

PERSIAN

These long-haired lovelies were first imported from Persia in the 1600s, although their true origins remain a mystery. Prized for their show-stopping good looks and natural elegance, they were a favourite of Queen Victoria, who had multiple Persians within her household, a fact which only added to their noble reputation.

Their distinctive flat faces make them instantly recognizable, but it wasn't always this way. A genetic mutation in the 1950s caused a batch of kittens to be born with this feature, and breeders decided to keep it. The silky hair is also a dominant characteristic, but it demands attention and grooming every day to keep it tangle free and glossy. Quiet in nature and equally attentive, the Persian likes to be adored, and will return the favour threefold to its human.

FELINE MYTH

GREEK MONSTERS AND MAYHEM

The ancient Greeks, like most nations, were fascinated by felines and also feared them, incorporating them into many of their most famous myths. The creatures they created were breathtaking and enigmatic, because of the cat-like influences they embodied.

The Chimera, the Sphinx and the Nemean Lion, also known as Leo, were three siblings sired by Typhon, a ghastly beast with a thousand dragons' heads. Their mother Echidna was part-woman, part-snake. Together, Typhon and Echidna brought the three siblings into creation, giving each one a feline element. The fearsome Chimera had the body and the head of a lion, and the hind quarters of either a dragon or a serpent. While the details varied, this awesome creature stalked the streets of Turkey, wreaking havoc until the hero Bellerophon and his trusty steed Pegasus slayed it. The Sphinx was equally terrifying, and clever too. With the body of a cat and the head of a woman, she set riddles to those who crossed her path, and when they couldn't answer, she would devour them on the spot. The Nemean Lion, so named because he prowled the hills of Nemea, was eventually slain by Hercules. The great god Zeus was so impressed with his feline strength that he cast his body into the sky to become the stunning constellation Leo.

CAT SUPERSTITION

TRAVELLING CATS

In superstitions all around the world, it was advised that sailors and those travelling across water keep a cat by their side. If their feline companion was black, then their journey would go smoothly. There were practical reasons for this: keeping a cat on board meant that rodents were less likely, and this in turn prevented disease, but there were also other, supernatural benefits.

Sailors believed that cats could control storms, and so the best way to appease them was to keep them happy and well-fed. They could also predict the weather by the cat's actions. If a cat licked its fur against the grain, then a hailstorm was on the way, but frisky, playful behaviour signified windy weather. If the ship's cat made a beeline for a sailor, this was fortuitous, and the recipient would be blessed with good fortune, but the opposite was true if the cat ran away.

CAT CHAT

EYE EYE

Cats' pupils contract and narrow to signal their emotions, but the quandary is in deciding whether they're angry, fearful or happy. A kitty's eyes will close to slits to signal an attack. The same can be said of a cat in defence mode, but this will usually be accompanied by hisses or growls. A happy cat will *also* squint in this way, and make a deep purring sound. Wide, staring eyes are a sign of excitement and interest, and if you should be blessed by a long slow blink, then the cat in question is saying, 'I love you.'

THE CAT'S WHISKERS

FELINE DREAMING

Staring into the middle distance, cats often appear lost in daydream, leaving cat parents to ponder about what they're thinking, and if they dream like us. The answer is yes. Like humans, when our felines drift into REM slumber, which usually happens every twenty minutes, they also enter the realm of dreams. Experts believe that the contents of these imaginings are based on their daily activities, and that they re-enact any exciting events they've experienced, such as chasing a butterfly, climbing a tree or snaffling a sausage from next door's barbecue. The average cat sleeps around fifteen hours a day, using the time to heal and recharge – that's a lot of dreams to be had!

CAT STRETCH

THE WALKING LUNGE

Cats like to stretch on the go, flexing their back legs as they stride forwards. With no time to spare, they make the most of each movement and use a couple of walking lunges to fire up their muscles. You can use a similar manoeuvre to boost your energy at any point during the day.

· Stand with your feet hip-width apart and your shoulders back. Lengthen your spine.

· Draw a deep breath in through both feet and lunge forwards with your right leg, bending as low as is comfortable for you.

· Feel the stretch along each leg and hold the position for a few seconds.

· As you release the breath, bring the other leg forwards and return to a standing position.

· Repeat the process with the opposite leg, lunging and then bringing the other leg forwards to meet it.

· Repeat twice more.

FELINE FUN

SCENT-SATIONAL KITTIES

Cats love your natural smell, and you will often find them drawn to items of clothing that you've worn. It's all about the scent and combining their unique whiff with yours to create a communal aroma that says, 'I belong to you, and you belong to me.' In doing so, they feel safe and secure, and this can help in situations where they are out of their comfort zone, like when they're in their carrier on the way to the vet. Keep an old unwashed T-shirt and let your cat sleep with it to create a tribal scent unique to you both, then pop this in the carrier when you're transporting them anywhere. You can also wrap it around them when dispensing a pill or giving them any kind of medical treatment.

CAT SPELL

SPELL TO HELP YOUR CAT FEEL MORE CONFIDENT

Some cats are bold and brave by nature, while others struggle with shyness, particularly when it comes to meeting new humans. This spell will help your feline be more open and trusting in social situations.

You will need: a small scoop of sunflower seeds, your cat's food bowl, a piece of tiger's eye

Perform this spell at midday on a Sunday, which is associated with the vibrant energy of the sun.

· Place the sunflower seeds in your cat's food bowl and carry it outside along with the piece of tiger's eye – this stone is associated with courage and vitality.

· Sit beneath the light of the midday sun and sprinkle some of the seeds in a circle on the grass. Place the tiger's eye in the middle of the circle.

· Say your cat's name three times, then add, 'May you find your stride and release the tiger inside.'

· Save a pinch of the remaining sunflower seeds, remove the shells and add the seeds to your cat's next meal. These nutritious seeds are packed with fibre and will benefit their digestive health, while boosting their confidence.

MAY

RUSSIAN BLUE

With shimmering grey coats and bright green eyes, this breed is renowned for its beauty and magical roots. Thought to have originated from Archangel in northern Russia where they scavenged the wilderness, the Russian Blue was a favourite of sailors, who would often take them aboard their ship. Sweet and affectionate, these clever cats – often called Archangel Blues – enjoy a challenge and plenty of room to hunt. They're also keen lap cats and can be shy in social situations.

The dense outercoat of this kitty is flecked with silvery hairs which make it sparkle in certain lights. It's no wonder it was the favoured breed of Russian royalty, who believed the Russian Blue had healing powers. This esteemed kitty was given a place to sleep in the royal nursery to protect little ones from evil, and attract good luck.

PUSS PREDICTIONS

It's a common belief that cats can predict pregnancy, and there are many superstitions surrounding this. According to Amish tradition, should you find a sleeping puss in an empty cradle, then there will be news of a new arrival, and if you want to conceive, then placing a cat *into* a cradle can help to make it happen. In Europe, it was a common belief that pregnant women should not let a cat lay upon their belly for fear that the child would be born with feline features, or a cat-shaped birthmark upon its face. Another strange superstition suggested that cats could suck the life from babies while they were sleeping.

THE CAT'S WHISKERS

FELINE SENSES

Cats are colour blind. They can recognize shades like blue and green – common in a cat's natural environment – but pink and bright red are a mystery to moggies, and purple tends to appear blue. While their eyes are more equipped to navigate the dark than ours, they lack vital colour-sensitive cells known as cones in each retina, which makes it hard for them to distinguish other hues in the spectrum. The same goes for their sense of taste. With only a few hundred taste buds, compared to the 9,000 we have, they are 'sweet-blind', and only able to appreciate savoury foods.

FELINE MYTH

SLAVIC CATS AND EVIL SPIRITS

In Slavic mythology, the feline was a thing of mystery, a powerful creature that could appear and disappear into thin air. Though prized by owners, cats cared little for their human family, except if there were children at home. Then they were fiercely protective, keeping evil spirits at bay and guarding the abode from invasion. Associated with Veles, the god of the underworld and cattle, cats were admired for their independent spirit and the freedom with which they travelled between worlds. Just like the god who governed them, they were considered nocturnal beings that liked to wander the dream realm.

The Slavic adoration of all things feline meant that anybody who dared to harm a hair upon their head would be blighted with seven years of bad luck. The belief was that in angering one cat, you incurred the wrath of all, which resulted in the removal of any protection, feline or otherwise. If a cat took a real dislike to you, it would bide its time and wait until the moment of death, when it would leap over your prone body and turn you into a vampire.

CAT CHAT

TELLING TAILS

A cat's tail acts like a thermometer, giving an instant reading of their mood. If their tail sticks straight up in the air, then the cat is pleased to see you; it's relaxed in its environment and happy with life. If the end quivers slightly, then the feline is feeling fabulous and experiencing a moment of pure pleasure. The opposite is true if the tail is pointing downwards. This kitty is feeling stressed and defensive. If the tail wraps around the body protectively, it's a sign of fear. A puffed-up tail that expands to twice its size is a signal of extreme agitation and aggression, and a non-verbal warning to keep your distance.

FELINE FUN

FIND THE TREAT

Cats love mental stimulation, so anything that piques their curiosity and gets them thinking will be a joy to watch. Throw in a reward like a biscuit or toy and you'll be their best human ever.

Find three identical paper cups and place a small toy mouse or ball inside one, then whizz the cups around in front of your cat. Let them watch as you alternate positions, then let your cat knock over the cups until they find the one with the toy inside. If you're looking to keep them on their toes and prevent them from eating too fast, you can hide a treat and make it a game. Take several pieces of scrunched-up paper and pop a biscuit inside one of them. Scatter the paper balls in every direction and watch your cat hunt for the treasure.

CAT STRETCH

THE PREY ROLL

This move is all about the win; it's that moment when your cat has the toy within its paws and is revelling in the victory. Emulate this and give the base muscles of your spine a gentle massage at the same time.

· Lie on your side with your arms stretched above your head, and your legs and toes pointed.

· Take a deep breath in and curl into a foetal position. Imagine you're a cat with a catnip mouse and bring your knees right up to your chest.

· Exhale and roll onto your back, staying in a tight ball.

· Rock from side to side, pushing your lower spine into the floor gently.

· To finish, take a breath in and roll onto the opposite side, then stretch your arms and legs out and repeat.

CAT SPELL

SPELL TO HELP YOU COMMUNICATE TELEPATHICALLY WITH YOUR CAT

Cats are naturally psychic. They instinctively pick up on atmospheres, unlike humans who often struggle to notice subtle shifts in energy. This magical technique will help you strengthen the psychic bond you have with your puss.

Lavender oil is not safe for kitties, so ensure you wash your hands thoroughly once you've finished the ritual.

You will need: an amethyst cluster, some lavender facial oil

Perform this spell on a Monday evening when the moon is waning. Mondays are associated with lunar power, which can strengthen psychic ability.

· Choose a moment when you and your cat are sitting quietly in each other's presence. You don't have to be touching. Place the cluster of amethyst between you.

· Add a tiny drop of the lavender facial oil to your fingers and gently massage it into your forehead in a circular motion. This will activate your third eye chakra, the energy centre associated with psychic ability.

- Gaze into your cat's eyes, or if they're not facing you, close your eyes and make a connection with them.

- Imagine a purple strand of light passing from your forehead to theirs. You can send messages along this strand and let them know how you feel.

- Start with something simple like telling them how much they mean to you, and that you'd really like to stroke them.

- Pour all your love into the message and imagine it passing between you. Then relax, breathe and see what happens. You might notice small changes like your cat's ears twitching, or they might reach out with a paw or move closer.

- Wash any lavender oil from your hands once the ritual is complete, and before touching your cat.

- Practise this exercise regularly to enhance your telepathic connection.

SUMMER

Suddenly the dewy, subtle warmth of spring is replaced by the fiery heat of summer. The sun turns up its blaze and the earth basks in its glory. Everything is bathed in brightness, from the flowers and trees to each creature, big and small. We become alight and awash with colour, and the same goes for our cats, for there is nothing they love more than to languish in the sunshine.

Lazy days filled with gentle play are the order of the day for our felines, and thanks to the temperature rise, they need less food in their bellies to sustain them. Should the heat become too much, you will find them seeking out cooler spots within your home, and conserving energy with a sneaky siesta. This is all part of their coping mechanism as the seasons shift. But while they'll love to lounge in the sun, there are dangers lurking too. Just like us, kitties can suffer sunburn, so a dab of protection upon their sensitive ears, pink noses and soft bellies will help, but be sure when you do this that you rub the mixture in well, and don't leave any excess oil on your cat's skin. A little sun lotion will allow them to sit amongst the greenery and sniff the roses.

JUNE

SCOTTISH FOLD

With their charming temperament and sweet nature, the Scottish Fold is a popular choice for those who want an easy-going kitty. Named for their distinctive ear folds, which can be single, double or triple, they also have round, owlish faces that accentuate their large glistening eyes. While cats with folded ears have been around since the 1700s, the Scottish Fold was first created in the 1960s, when a kitten called Susie was born into a litter of non-folded felines in Perthshire, Scotland. This beguiling barn cat with white fur and quirky bent ears instantly struck a chord, and so she was bred with other cats to recreate the look.

The signature ear folds develop eighteen to twenty-four days after birth, and as the unique look is a genetic mutation, Scottish Folds are never bred together, as this would cause degenerative health issues. There is always one parent with straight ears and one with a fold, producing litters that have a 50 per cent chance of developing this characteristic.

CAT SUPERSTITION

THEATRICAL CATS

From the graceful way they move to their dramatic and often ostentatious behaviour, there's something theatrical about cats, and this has influenced many superstitions. It's a common belief that a cat in a theatre brings good luck, particularly if it should bless the stage on opening night. Traditionally, this might have been for its ability to keep vermin under control, though according to folklore, it's down to its supernatural powers. An auspicious symbol, the cat keeps evil spirits at bay and attracts good energy into the building. If one should run across the stage mid-performance, then the show is well starred, but should an actor accidentally kick the moggy mid-monologue, bad luck will follow.

CAT CHAT

SOUND BITES

Cats are chatty and can make over a hundred different vocal sounds. From the velvety vibrations of a contented purr – created by the vocal chords rattling together – to the gentle chirrup, these sounds are used to get the attention of both humans and other cats. The chatter – an open-mouthed, repetitive clicking noise – is usually made when a feline has spotted some prey in the distance. It signals excitement and frustration that they can't reach it. The simple miaow comes in a range of styles, from 'feed me' to 'stroke me', or 'please don't touch me!' Cats use it specifically with humans as a way to communicate their needs.

THE PERUVIAN DEMON CAT

Where the swirling mists of the Peruvian Andes meet the sky, in amongst the shadows, you might see the fearsome Ccoa lurking. A creature of legend, according to the Quechua tribe, this cat-like spirit stalks the earth in search of mischief. While it isn't entirely malevolent, it does have an evil streak, and when threatened will arch its enormous back and spit hail. Generous in size, the Ccoa has charcoal-grey fur marked by horizontal black stripes, and enormous glowing eyes that shoot bolts of lightning. This feline also has the ability to fly through the heavens and control storms, and should you experience a sudden downpour, it's likely that the Ccoa is urinating in your direction.

To appease this creature, local farmers leave offerings in the hope that their crops will not be destroyed by bad weather. While this works for the most part, the Ccoa is unpredictable and has lent its power to sorcerers. Believed to be the pet of the mountain gods, this kitty is not a plaything, and demands a degree of respect amongst the locals.

THE CAT'S WHISKERS

WALKING ON THE WILD SIDE

Cats have a lot in common with their big cat cousins, sharing 95.6 per cent of their DNA. This goes some way to explaining their wild side. While the domestic kitty may seem more docile than the average tiger, there are many similarities, from their body shape and structure to the way they mark and protect their territory. This, coupled with their ability to survive and thrive in almost any situation, makes your miniature panther a true marvel. Thanks to their ancestral roots, cats can easily endure the dusty, lifeless heat of a desert environment, conserving water by sweating through their pores, while feasting on raw meat. Even the extra bit of tummy flab they carry has a purpose. It adds a further layer of protection against their vital organs should they get into a scrap with a neighbourhood cat.

CAT STRETCH

THE BOTTOM WIGGLE

If you've ever seen your cat in hunting mode, you'll recognize this move. It's the little wiggle they do while getting into the perfect position to pounce. It's also a great way to free up hip joints and relax lower-back muscles.

· Kneel on all fours with your forearms and hands flat to the floor.

· Keep your back flat and your head gazing forwards.

· Take a deep breath in and tighten your tummy muscles.

· Hold for a count of four, then release and gently wiggle your hips in a slow side-to-side motion.

· Try to keep your bottom still and feel the stretch along your spine.

· When you're ready, roll back onto your legs until you are in a kneeling position.

· Elongate your spine, tilt your chin upwards and take another deep breath to finish.

FELINE FUN

KITTY WORKOUT

Appeal to your cat's sense of fun by creating an obstacle course. You don't need to invest in anything special – just use objects you have to hand that are safe for your cat to climb over, such as cushions, tables and stools. You can also appeal to your cat's love of cardboard boxes by taping together a collection to create a tunnel for them to run through. Create even more fun by cutting kitty-sized windows into the cardboard tunnel. Once you've amassed a selection of objects for your cat to navigate, encourage them to explore by hiding their favourite toy somewhere in the course, or using a feather on a stick as a lure that they can chase.

CAT SPELL

SPELL TO SOOTHE YOUR CAT'S NERVES BEFORE A TRIP TO THE VET

Cats have a magical ability to sense when something is afoot, particularly a trip to the vet. If your kitty gets super stressed whenever they see their carrier, this spell will help to calm them down before and during the journey.

You will need: a piece of moonstone, your cat's carrier, lavender essential oil, geranium essential oil, a small bowl of warm water

Perform this spell the night before a trip to the vet, or in the morning, an hour before you have to leave.

· Take the moonstone and hold it over your heart.

· Close your eyes, take a couple of long deep breaths, and then say, 'Let the love in my heart soothe your fears away. Let peace surround you in every way.'

· Place the moonstone on top of your cat's carrier. Moonstone has a gentle energy that helps to settle emotions.

· Sprinkle four drops of lavender essential oil and three drops of geranium essential oil into the bowl of warm water. Lavender is known for its relaxing properties, and geranium is uplifting.

· Place this on a table and sit and inhale the lavender scent to relax your aura. While your cat shouldn't breathe in these oils, they will pick up on the calmness of your energy and relax.

· Remove the bowl and keep the moonstone in your pocket so that it's in close proximity to both you and your cat during the trip to the vet.

JULY

BENGAL

Highly active and intelligent, the beautiful Bengal is a muscular powerhouse of a cat. Sleek and sporty, with distinctive marbled fur, it was originally bred from the Asian Leopard and a domestic short hair back in 1963.

Favoured for its feral appearance, the Bengal is a big softy that loves to play, chase and interact with its human family. Its shimmering patterned coat comes in a range of shades from golden brown to rust and chocolate. Coupled with its round, owlish face and large, glistening eyes, this stunning feline could easily prowl the catwalk. It would also be at home in the jungle, thanks to its high energy levels and adventurous spirit. Like its wildcat ancestor, this puss is a huge fan of water and enjoys taking a dip, so don't be surprised if it follows you into the shower!

THE CAT'S WHISKERS

PAW POWER

Cats are right- or left-pawed, just like humans are right- or left-handed. Whether they're swiping a prawn from the BBQ, or tapping you on the head when you're not paying them enough attention, there's a paw they'll favour the most. Male cats are usually lefties, while females tend to go for their right side. Cats can also be nail-biters! A little claw chewing is perfectly normal, though if you notice your cat obsessively nipping at its paws there might be an underlying reason. Nail-biting in cats is a nervous reaction and can be a sign of anxiety or boredom. Spending time with your kitty and ensuring they are fully entertained with toys and games should put an end to this habit.

CAT SUPERSTITION

KITTEN BLESSINGS

Kittens are a wonderful omen wherever you are in the world, which is not surprising. How could tiny bundles of cuteness not symbolize good fortune? It's particularly lucky if they're born in your home and you may be blessed with a windfall, or prosperity of some kind, within three months. If the kittens in question are black, then this only increases the luck, and in Latvia, this is a sign you'll have a good harvest. Should the kittens be born in the month of May, they will be gifted magical powers and considered witch's cats, and have the ability to keep evil spirits at bay. It's generally thought that if a cat chooses to have her kittens in your home, then it's ghost free. Some traditions state that a mother cat must move her litter seven times after they are first born, otherwise their eyes will never fully open.

FELINE MYTH

THE TIGER AND THE CAT

In Indonesian folklore, the cat was thought to be the king of all the animals. According to one legend, there was a time when all creatures lived together in harmony and could talk like humans. They chose the cat to be their leader because he was clever and gifted, and willing to share his wisdom. The tiger was the cat's most dedicated pupil. He wanted to learn everything, but most of all he wanted to know how the cat could climb trees. The cat didn't entirely trust the tiger, and so he taught him everything except how to climb trees. He showed him how to swim, how to crawl and sneak quietly through the undergrowth, but never how to climb.

Eventually the tiger grew angry and asked why the cat would not reveal his secret. The cat, being honest in nature, said that he felt the tiger might use it to do something bad. The tiger was enraged and chased the cat through the jungle and almost caught him, but he escaped by climbing the tallest of trees. The tiger could not follow, and so he threatened that one day he would steal the cat's power by eating his faeces. This is the reason why all cats bury their poop: they do not want a tiger to steal their magic.

FELINE FIDGETS

Movement is the key to kitty communication. Watching what they do and when they do it will give you an idea of what's going through your cat's mind. Kneading, also fondly referred to as 'making biscuits', is the steady pummelling action that cats do with their front paws, usually on a soft surface such as their bed or blanket, or even your lap. It's a sign your cat is happy and relaxed, and getting ready to settle down for a snooze. This behaviour is something tiny kittens do when they are suckling to stimulate milk flow from their mum, and it's a natural instinct that is often carried into adulthood. A similar action can be done with the back paws, but it's usually more forceful. Rear paw treading is a sign your cat is fired up, and is often performed before or after mating, or when an attack is imminent!

CAT STRETCH

THE CROUCHING TABBY

This manoeuvre can be tricky because you are not built the same as a cat and don't have the gift of feline elasticity, but it's a great glute workout, and will also improve your flexibility and general get-up-and-go. The key is to take your time and have fun with this.

· Stand with your feet slightly apart and your shoulders relaxed.

· Look straight ahead and take a deep breath, tighten your tummy muscles, and squat down into a crouching position.

· Your knees should be bent and your weight slightly forwards on the balls of your feet. You can use your hands or fingertips to steady yourself so that you don't tip forwards.

· Continue to breathe naturally through the rest of the exercise.

· Bounce lightly in this position, and when you're ready, spring up into a standing position again.

· Don't worry if you wobble when you drop to the floor or as you spring up. This is perfectly normal and you will become more flexible and graceful with practice.

FELINE FUN

CAT NAPPING

While cats like to be entertained, they also appreciate the joy of an impromptu nap. Sleep is an important part of their daily schedule. It allows them to rest, recharge and daydream. Make the most of this sedentary time to bond with your cat. Sit with them and enjoy the silence. Meditate, or if you prefer, simply focus on your breathing and slow it right down so that it's in time with the rise and fall of your cat's tummy. This helps to relax them even more, as they will pick up on your chilled vibes. You might want to try some gentle stroking to soothe your feline into sleep, or turn your hand to something more creative, such as drawing a picture of them or writing a poem. They will appreciate the attention, and you will enjoy the challenge.

CAT SPELL

SPELL TO MAKE FRIENDS WITH ANY CAT

From new cats on the block to the stray that's been hanging around your back door, it's not always easy to gain a feline's trust. Repeat this spell several times over a few weeks to make lifelong fur friends.

You will need: a yellow candle, a lighter or matches, dried catnip, a feather, a length of wool

Perform this spell on a Sunday at any point during the day when the sun is shining, as this boosts positive energy.

· Light the yellow candle and sprinkle the catnip around it in a circular pattern to represent the never-ending cycle of friendship. Yellow promotes joy and understanding.

· Take the feather in both hands and say, 'Love and light, between us flows. With every day our friendship grows.'

· Tie the length of wool to the stem of the feather and let the candle burn down.

· The next time you see a cat you'd like to get to know, use the dangling feather toy you have made to entice it closer. Build upon the trust between you with a moment of play.

AUGUST

SPHYNX

This enigmatic breed may get their name from the Great Sphinx of Giza, but their unique appearance belies a sweet and loving nature. Although they look hairless, on closer inspection you'll discover that these cats are covered with a downy layer of fur, which feels like suede. Despite this, they do get cold and will need to wear clothes and have plenty of snuggle spots when the temperature drops.

Their sensitive skin needs careful attention. Like most felines, it secretes oil, which would normally keep a dense coat smooth, but in hairless breeds the oil creates a thin film of grease, which means these kitties benefit from a weekly bath. They're also in danger of getting sunburnt, which is why the Sphynx is generally an indoor cat. They might seem high maintenance, but this striking puss is a sociable softy that loves to be around its owner and gets easily depressed if left for long periods of time. Believed to be symbols of good fortune, the Sphynx is associated with wealth and prosperity.

THE CAT'S WHISKERS

FELINE FLEXIBILITY

Cats have super-flexible spines: their vertebrae have special cushioned discs between them, which work like elastic and allow the cat to rotate its torso up to 180 per cent to the left or right. In comparison, humans can only rotate by up to 90 per cent. Cats also have malleable muscles. This, coupled with loose shoulders, which are only attached to the torso by muscles rather than forming a part of the joint, mean that felines have the ability to take huge running leaps and crawl into the tiniest of gaps.

CAT SUPERSTITION

TABBY TALES

Tabby cats have their own folklore, which makes them extra special. Like black cats, they are associated with good luck, but also linked to the supernatural and witches. In the Middle Ages in Europe, it was believed that tabby cats had the power to transform into a horse for the witch to ride through the night. Thought to have the oldest coat pattern in the feline world, their striking markings make them stand out. The characteristic M shape, which is said to represent the sacred scarab beetle in Egyptian folklore, is also a reference to Mau, their Egyptian name. Others believe it's associated with the Muslim prophet Mohammed, who left the distinctive mark as a blessing after the cat warned him of imminent danger. The dark stripes along its back are where the prophet stroked the friendly kitty.

FELINE MYTH

THE EGYPTIAN CAT GODDESS

Beautiful and beguiling, the Egyptian cat-headed goddess Bastet was a favourite with the people. A keen advocate for women, she took her role as protectress seriously, especially when it came to felines. Daughter of the sun god Ra and associated with both the sun and the moon, Bastet was linked to the All Seeing Eye. Every day she would accompany Ra as he journeyed through the sky on his chariot. It was her responsibility to keep both him and his burning orb safe from the clutches of the evil serpent demon Apep.

With a mass of ardent followers, Bastet's teachings were taken to heart by her people, who believed in the sacred power of the puss. It was therefore illegal to harm a hair upon the head of any cat, and anyone who dared would be punished with death. Cats within the home were loved and honoured, even after death: family members would shave off their eyebrows as a mark of respect for their deceased kitty. They were often mummified along with the rest of the family and buried with numerous treasures and toys to entertain them as they passed on to the next life.

CAT CHAT

KITTY CLOSENESS

Cats rub against you to express their love. In feline speak it's a way of taking ownership and saying, 'You're mine.' They are using the scent glands in their face, lips and chin to mark their territory. Licking, too, is a sign of affection, and a way of strengthening the bond between you. Surprisingly, if a cat nibbles or gently bites you, it is also a sign of love. It's a behaviour learnt from kittenhood. When mum lovingly cleans and grooms her babies she licks, nibbles and often delicately nips at their fur to keep it in tip-top condition. If your cat spends time licking and playfully biting, then it's clearly saying, 'You're a part of my crew and I love you.'

CAT STRETCH

THE FOETAL ROLL

This manoeuvre is something cats do instinctively when they're settling down after a busy day of catching flies. It's a series of movements that will help you relax and unwind, so it's perfect to practise at the end of the day when you want to release stress and slow down.

- Lie on your side and breathe slowly and deeply.

- Gradually bring your legs up to your chest in a foetal position.

- Curl into yourself and feel the comfort that this position brings. Notice how the ground supports you and take a moment to enjoy this feeling.

- Take a couple of deep breaths and roll over onto your other side in this position.

- Breathe, relax, and slowly unfurl your legs and body until you're lying on your side.

- Repeat this cycle three times.

FELINE FUN

BALLS AND BOXES

Balls and boxes are the perfect pairing for your cat, allowing their natural curiosity and sense of fun to take over. Ping-pong balls are light and easy to bat around. Pop a couple in an empty bath and watch your kitty scoot around after them. The shape and smooth surface of the bath acts like an ice rink, allowing the balls to roll in every direction. If you have an empty shoebox, cut a series of paw-sized holes in the lid and the sides. Add a few balls inside, stick the lid on and shake the box to generate interest, then watch as your cat attempts to hunt the balls inside by sticking its paw into the different holes. This also works with automated toys which you can release in the box.

CAT SPELL

SPELL TO HELP YOUR CAT GET USED TO A NEW HOME

Moving home is stressful, and even more so for your cat who doesn't understand what is going on. It can take time for them to acclimatize, but this spell should help them feel more relaxed in their new environment.

You will need: fresh sage leaves, sage essential oil, a small bowl half-filled with warm water, a bell

Perform this spell the night before you move in, or once you're in your new home.

· Add a handful of sage leaves and three or four drops of sage essential oil to the bowl of warm water. Sage has cleansing and uplifting properties.

· Walk around the rooms in your new abode carrying the bowl so that the aroma fills each space. As you do this, imagine a white light sweeping through each room, clearing away any residual negative energy.

· Discard the water, away from where your cat can drink it, then place the bowl in the central living space. Walk through your home with the bell. As you enter each room, shake the bell and say, 'This is a safe space for me and my fur family.'

· Give your cat time to get used to their new surroundings and leave lots of blankets and toys dotted around to help them feel comfortable.

AUTUMN

The powerful, all-encompassing heat of the summer is swifty swapped for the zing of autumn freshness. There's a nip to the air that pinches the cheeks and imbues each step with zest, for while the temperature drops, the trees and plants respond with gusto. Their leaves turn to burnished amber and gold and fall to form a crisp carpet on the ground. It is a whole new world for the curious cat. With a plethora of treats that come in all shapes and sizes, from acorns and pine cones, to berries and nuts, it must seem like the heavens have opened and showered the earth in an array of wondrous gifts. It's no wonder some cats receive a second wind during the autumn months as there is so much to see, explore and experience.

But while wide-eyed kitties make the most of this transition, they too go through changes. Their coat begins to shed its summer softness, and their furry underlayer gets thicker in preparation for the big chill, making furballs a common feature at this time of year. Regular grooming with a brush will help your cat make the most of their new autumn garb and help them look and feel their best.

SEPTEMBER

BURMESE

With looks and charm, it's easy to see why the Burmese is such a popular cat breed. Like its name, which is Thai for 'beautiful, fortunate and of splendid appearance', this feline has always known how to strike a pose. When an American sailor travelled back from Burma with one of these adorable kitties as his travel companion, the breed's fate was sealed. The cat, a walnut brown beauty called Wong Mau, was given to Dr Joseph Thompson, a renowned Siamese breeder who was so taken with the cat's exotic appearance that he decided to breed his prize Siamese with it. The resulting litter are the ancestors of the modern Burmese.

With roundish features and a solid sturdy build, this cat is quite the heavyweight when it comes to size. It has a short glossy coat which comes in a range of colours, although sable brown is the traditional hue. Super friendly and fun, it loves to engage with the world. From being involved in family life to window gazing, this puss likes to take everything in, and be at the heart of the action.

CAT SUPERSTITION

WHITE CATS

It's usually black cats that are associated with luck; however, white cats also have their share of quirky superstitions. In general, they're a fortunate omen: a white coat symbolizes purity and innocence. It's thought that if one crosses your path you should treat it with kindness, and you'll be blessed with good fortune for the rest of the day.

In Russia, white cats are synonymous with money, and if one chooses to visit you and enters your home, then you can expect a sudden influx of cash. In the UK, this belief is reversed; it's a sign that things are about to get financially difficult – although if the same cat leaves promptly, then the bad luck leaves with them. In the Mediterranean, if a white cat takes a liking to a child, then they will grow up to achieve great things!

THE CAT'S WHISKERS

FELINE FALLING

Cats are the superheroes of the animal kingdom. They have the ability to jump six times their own body length, and can fall just as far and still land gracefully on all fours. Even if they do take a tumble from a great height, it's unlikely they'll do any serious damage, thanks to the fact that their body has a large surface area compared to their weight. This reduces the force of impact when they hit the ground. Cool cats also know not to panic, and use the time spent falling to prepare for their landing.

FELINE MYTH

PUSSY WILLOWS

In Poland, the cat is revered and believed to keep evil spirits at bay. It's seen as a fortunate omen and features in many traditional tales. One popular story tells of a litter of kittens who were chasing butterflies by the river one spring morning. Being so engrossed in their game, they didn't notice they were dangerously close the water's edge, and fell in. The mother cat tried desperately to reach them, but it was too late. The flow of the river was powerful and the kittens were carried further away. All the mother cat could do was watch and wail at the sight of her tiny fluff balls bobbing in the water.

Luckily the nearby willows heard her plaintiff cries and stretched their slender branches out towards the kittens, who one by one clung to the swarthy stems. The babies were swiftly pulled to safety, and peace was restored. As a mark of respect to the elegant willows and a nod to the magical nature of the cat, each spring, the willows sprout fuzzy, furry little buds that grip tightly to the branches to represent the adorable kittens that were saved from a watery death.

CAT CHAT

FELINE FITNESS

Cats are clever at disguising how they really feel. In the wild, if a cat is injured or sick it covers it up, as it would be dangerous to show any sign of weakness when faced with predators. Domesticated moggies are less likely to do this, but they can be stoic, so it's important to know what to look for, and to read your cat's body language. Sick felines often lie down or sit hunched, and will shy away from touch. You may also notice that they're grooming less. If your feline is in pain, it will limit its movement, and that includes trips to the litter tray, or to eat and drink. You may hear it purring, but do not confuse this with feeling joyful. Purring is an automatic response to pleasure *and* pain, and can be your cat's way of saying, 'Help me.'

CAT STRETCH

THE ARCHED CAT

This is a favourite feline stretch and one that cats perform on a daily basis. It flexes the muscles around the spine and the shoulder blades, keeping them subtle and relaxed. As humans, we recognize the benefits of this kitty manoeuvre and have even incorporated this move into our yoga practice. Practise this move whenever your shoulders need a deep massage.

- Begin on all fours with your back flat, your hips over your knees, and your hands shoulder-distance apart.

- Take a deep breath in and press your hands down into the floor.

- Exhale and round your spine, tuck your tummy in, and let your tailbone and head fall towards the floor.

- Let your neck relax and spread your shoulder blades to release any tension by pushing deeply into the floor with your hands.

- Hold this position for a few seconds, then relax and return to the starting position.

FELINE FUN

PUSS PAMPERING

Grooming is an essential part of your cat's routine and takes up 30–50 per cent of their time. You might think all this pampering is excessive, but it promotes blood flow, distributes the natural oils throughout the coat and keeps kitty cool when the temperatures rise. It's also extremely enjoyable for both cat and human. Get in on the act by investing in a brush or comb, and taking the time to stroke and fuss over your feline. Consider it an exercise in bonding, and help your cat feel comfortable by including a few of their favourite treats to keep them calm and satisfied while you brush. You could also put on some relaxing music to help them feel soothed.

CAT SPELL

SPELL TO BRING YOUR CAT GOOD LUCK

There's no denying that felines are furry packages of joy. They melt the heart, raise the spirits and are good for your health. But even cats can have their share of bad luck. From misadventures on their travels to feline face-offs and sticking their nose into all the wrong places, some kitties seem to attract trouble. This spell helps to flip the scales and turn luck in their favour.

You will need: a white candle, a lighter or matches, a piece of paper, a pen with gold or silver ink, a fireproof dish

Perform this spell on a Thursday, when the planet Jupiter's positive influence can be felt.

· Light the white candle and spend a few minutes gazing into the flame. White is the colour of purity and has cleansing properties, so it can help to wipe the slate clean and attract positive energy.

· Write your cat's name in the sparkling ink on the piece of paper.

· Write a wish for good fortune beneath their name, such as, 'Bless my cat with good luck!'

· Fold the paper three times and say, 'By the power of three, so it will be.'

· Pass the paper through the flame of the candle and drop it into the fireproof dish to burn down.

· Let the candle burn down.

· Scatter the paper ash in the bin and repeat your magical request.

OCTOBER

CAT OF THE MONTH

BIRMAN

First recognized as a breed in France in 1925, the Birman, also known as the Sacred Cat of Burma, is a colourful beauty. Its creamy luxurious coat and darker-toned face, tail and legs make it stand out from the crowd. Combine this with pure white gloves and socks, and a pair of peepers as blue as the azure ocean, and you have a cat worth looking at!

Selective breeding means this laidback lovely is made for family life, being both sociable and easy-going. Not one to steal the limelight on purpose, the Birman is quietly chatty and extremely affectionate, but if you really want to know the secret to its charm, spend a few minutes eye to eye. According to legend, the Birman was gifted its sapphire irises from a goddess who wanted to reward the kitty for its devotion to the temple priest. She also turned its thick coat golden, but left the paws white as a symbol of purity.

FELINE MYTH

JAMAICAN SPOOKS AND CAT SORCERY

Cats have always been linked to the supernatural, but in Jamaican folklore, they were seen as sinister and darkly powerful beings. Gifted with the ability to inflict their will on others, their magic was harnessed by using various body parts in spells and charms. It was common practice for an obeah man or woman (a type of spell-casting sorcerer) to use feline teeth or claws to set a curse upon another. The type of curse varied, but it might include placing the cat's incisor or nail beneath the skin to cause illness. Along with feathers and fishbones, cat's claws and teeth were often hung over doors to protect the home from theft.

In addition to their use in black magic, cats were popular with duppies too. These ghostly spirits could take on many forms, but their most terrifying was that of a giant tabby cat. In this shape, the duppy (known as the Rollin' Calf for its malevolent and feral nature) would terrorize the neighbourhood, causing chaos wherever it roamed.

SUPERNATURAL CATS

Animal familiars have always been associated with witches, and while any creature could take on this mantle, it was the mysterious moggy that really captured the imagination. Black was usually the chosen colour, but any type of feline could assume the role of a witch's familiar, as long as it was evil at heart, and prepared to serve the Devil. Some witch hunters believed that cats were Satan in furry guise, and a way for witches to communicate with the dark lord. Their independent nature and ability to hunt at night only served to support this theory, and the fact that their owners seemed to dote on their every move suggested they had succumbed to the cat's wicked ways. Some physicians even claimed that a cat's breath could putrefy the lungs, while others blamed them for the spread of the Great Plague.

CLEVER CATS

There are many reasons why cats are top of the class when it comes to street smarts. Their brain may only be the size of your pinkie finger and lighter than that of a new-born baby, but it is similar in structure to the human brain and gifted with 250 million cells – roughly the same as a brown bear. Humans have a larger pre-frontal cortex that means we can plan, remember and carry out complex behaviours, but cats have a much larger cerebellum, which gives them superb balance, body awareness and co-ordination for navigating the environment with ease. Cats are also gifted with a keen sense of recall and can distinguish between voices to pick out their human. Whether they choose to listen is another matter!

CAT CHAT

FELINE GIFTING

A dead rodent, spider or bird might not be what you had in mind for your birthday, but when your cat brings you this gift, it's actually a demonstration of their love. They're saying, 'You're part of my crew, so this is for you.' Despite being domesticated over 10,000 years ago, felines still have the urge to hunt and pass on these skills to their nearest and dearest, and that means their human too. This is even more prevalent in female cats, who are primed to educate their young in the ways of feline-hood. Your cat knows you're not a natural when it comes to catching prey, so they give you a helping paw because they want you to survive. After all, who would operate the tin-opener in your absence?

CAT STRETCH

THE BACKWARD STRETCH

This gentle manoeuvre is one you'll have seen often if your cat likes to lounge on the bed. It's extremely relaxing, while also helping to lengthen your spine and alleviate neck tension. No wonder it's a popular puss pose.

· Lie on your bed with your feet pointing towards the pillows.

· Keep your arms by your sides and let your head gently hang off the end of the bed. Your neck and upper body should be supported by the mattress.

· Take a long deep breath in and as you exhale, let the air seep from your lips slowly.

· Relax your body into the softness of the bed.

· Close your eyes and feel the stretch all the way along your spine through to the base of your skull.

· Soften your tummy and limbs.

· Keep deep breathing, focusing on the gentle stretch and letting each part of your body relax.

FELINE FUN

CAT AND MOUSE

Exercise is key to a happy feline. It keeps them fit and healthy, and also stimulated, which helps with anxiety and behavioural problems. Get your kitty moving and join in with the fun so you both benefit. A simple chasing game is lots of fun and builds the bond between you. Use a feather toy as a teaser or take a length of ribbon or an old scarf and use it as a lure while you run around the house and/or garden. If you prefer, tempt them with a game of football. Use a small, soft ball and knock it towards your cat to get them engaged. They'll soon get the hang of the game if you tap it forwards and back between you, then increase the distance of each kick to get them running.

CAT SPELL

SPELL TO TAP INTO YOUR CAT'S PSYCHIC POWERS

Who doesn't want a heads-up on future events? Your cat can help you predict the future using its sixth sense in this magical spell that's a fun game for them.

You will need: three sheets of paper, a marker pen, a piece of amethyst

Perform this spell on a Monday when the moon is at the height of its powers to boost your cat's intuitive senses and strengthen the connection between you.

· Write the words YES, NO and MAYBE on separate pieces of paper.

· Wait until your cat is relaxed and you are together.

· Place the amethyst between you on the floor to promote the flow of psychic energy.

· Relax, breathe deeply, and think of a question that you'd like an answer to, like, 'Will I win the lottery in the next month?'

· Screw each bit of paper into a ball and place them in a row in front of your cat.

· Say, 'May fate and fortune come to me, through my cat's psychic energy.' Then wait to see which paper ball your cat is drawn to first.

· If they don't make a move, encourage them by throwing the balls, and see which one the cat chases.

NOVEMBER

CAT OF THE MONTH

CORNISH REX

Svelte and leggy with an exceptionally long tail, the Cornish Rex is the greyhound of the feline world. Its large, enquiring eyes appear too big for its slim egg-shaped face, while huge bat-like ears only add to the whimsy. Combine this with a tight-knit curly coat, and you have a cat that is unique and charming in appearance and attitude.

These kitties, which hail from England and first emerged in the 1950s, have an enormous sense of fun. They love to play and are incredibly sociable. It is thought that the Cornish Rex came into being when a kitten was born to a British Shorthair with a genetic mutation that gave it super-long limbs and a curly coat. Named Kallibunker, it was then re-bred and over the years the genetic pool widened to establish the breed. Unlike most other cats, the Cornish Rex doesn't have three layers of fur: instead, there is only an undercoat to keep it warm. As a result, it's likely to feel the chill in winter, and is also susceptible to the heat, so needs extra care and attention during the changing seasons.

THE RAAS ISLAND MASCOT

The Raas Island of Indonesia is home to an indigenous domestic cat breed with a mysterious reputation, known as the Raas or the Madura, which means 'blue cat' and is so named for the blue-black sheen of its fur. This feline is blessed with a square-ish face, slender tapered chin and a large, muscular body, like that of the Bobcat. Gifted with a sixth psychic sense, this cat brings wealth and good luck, especially if it takes a liking to you and your home.

Should it ever leave the island, a change in fortunes would occur, and the one who took it would be doomed for an eternity. It's believed that the Raas can sink a ship with the blink of one of its gleaming green eyes. Should the sailors survive, they will be blighted to a life of misfortune, thanks to the wrath of this kitty. Because it's so esteemed, only high-ranking officials can keep the Raas. Even more revered is the Amethyst Raas, a sacred feline with a cinnamon coat, and a rare find amongst the island's population. If one of these crosses your threshold, you'll be blessed for life.

CAT SUPERSTITION

CATS AND THE SPIRIT REALM

Cats have long been admired for their ability to sense what cannot be seen and predict the future. In the British Isles, it was a common belief that if a cat should leave the home while their owner was stricken ill, it was a sign that they'd soon pass into the spirit world. A recently deceased corpse was never left in the company of a cat, for fear it might leap over the body, causing the person's soul to suffer unbelievable torment. In some homes this was taken to the extreme and cats were placed beneath inverted tubs as a way to prevent this from happening. Two cats fighting by the side of a fresh grave are thought to be an angel and the Devil at war over the person's soul, and should a cat sit happily staring into the distance while purring ferociously, it's likely it has spotted a ghost.

THE CAT'S WHISKERS

PSYCHIC KITTIES

Cats can predict natural disasters such as earthquakes and volcanic eruptions, according to scientific research. While it might sound ridiculous, these theories have been tried and tested, and have proved that cats have the ability to sense the subtle shifts that occur within the atmosphere and the Earth's magnetic field. Researchers believe that felines can feel the minimal tremors that are not perceptible to humans, with some even suggesting that cats detect the ions created when the planet's underground plates rub together. According to the evidence, cats become twitchy and restless at the first sign of a quake or an eruption, with some wailing in distress to warn their owners. Witnesses even report felines fleeing homes en masse in search of a safe place to hide.

CAT CHAT

SLEEP POSES

Your cat loves to nap, and it does this with typical feline flair in a variety of positions. The way your cat sleeps reveals how it feels and relates to its environment. A curled-up kitty is trying to preserve body heat, and also protect its vulnerable organs from attack. It's not threatened, it's just feeling the need to retreat and conserve energy. A cat flat on its back is a truly joyful sight. This puss is totally relaxed and feels safe and comfortable with its belly and all those essential organs exposed. A cat that is shaped like a loaf of bread with front paws tucked under is in nap mode. Alert enough to jump to action should the fridge door open, this kitty is chilled, and skilled in the art of grabbing forty winks.

FELINE FUN

QUIZ YOUR CAT

Cats are smart. They catch on quickly and adapt their behaviour to fit in with their human. But just how intelligent is your kitty? You can find out by conducting some simple tests. According to research, our felines have an understanding of object permanence, which means they know that something exists, even when it disappears from sight. Test this theory by taking their favourite toy. Let them sniff it and see it in your hands, then hide it behind the sofa. See if they look for it, and how quickly they retrieve it. You can check if you have a problem-solving puss by placing a treat in an egg carton. Clever cats will open the box in no time – though real moggie masterminds will wait for you to do it for them!

CAT STRETCH

THE BUTTERFLY STRETCH

Cats are spontaneous. They will leap, stretch and twist to achieve their aim. Always prepared for action, they seemingly spring to life when they're at their most relaxed. While we might not be able to jump from our beds with such gusto, a few gentle bounces can provide a quick energy boost.

- Stand with your feet hip-width apart and your shoulders relaxed.

- Take a deep breath in and raise up onto your toes.

- Bounce lightly in this position. Exhale, keeping your weight on your toes.

- Raise your arms above your head and push up through the balls of your feet. Imagine you're trying to catch a ball, or an errant butterfly that is fluttering above your head.

- Continue to breathe deeply as you reach upwards.

- Feel the stretch along your spine and tighten your core muscles as you bounce.

- Relax and return to a standing position, then repeat three times.

- Each time you repeat, try to stretch a little further with your arms and legs.

CAT SPELL

SPELL TO CALM YOUR CAT DURING FIREWORK SEASON

Fireworks can be a nightmare for anxious cats. If your feline is fearful of the loud sounds, this spell could help them cope.

You will need: calming music, a piece of rose quartz, a small bowl, two or three chamomile teabags, some hot water

Perform this spell in the lead-up to and during bonfire night.

- Choose a gentle piece of music and put it on in the room where your cat is. Classical music or nature sounds work well. Position the rose quartz next your cat.

- Place the teabags in the bowl. Half-fill the bowl with the hot water, and position it on a shelf high up in the same room so that the scented vapours fill the air. Chamomile is renowned for its soothing properties.

- Sit with your cat and relax. You might want to repeat a chant such as, 'All is well, all is calm.'

WINTER

The land steals itself for the onset of winter. The vibrant glow of autumn is quietly muted, dulled by the bitter chill that this season brings, and the animal kingdom follows suit. Retreating within, creatures nestle in the belly of the Earth and use this time to recharge. Our domestic cats are no different: their tender paws dislike the feel of icy ground, and they seek solace and warmth inside, finding treasured snuggle spots by the fire or on their human's lap.

It may seem that cats sleep more during colder months, but this is a natural reaction to the dimming of light, coupled with the need to conserve energy and heat. Food, too, becomes more essential, a basic need which harks back to a time when they had to forage and hunt for their dinner. It must have been slim pickings for their wild ancestors, trying to source a meal beneath a layer of snow and brittle soil. It's no wonder that today's felines place so much store upon their next snack, and only natural that they might gain some weight as they watch and wait for the return of the sun.

DECEMBER

MAINE COON

This gentle giant is often referred to as the dog of the cat world, and just like its canine counterpart, it's super-friendly, affectionate and loyal. The largest domestic cat breed in the world, Maine Coons can reach up to 1 metre (40in) tall and weigh in at a massive 8 kilograms (18lb). This, coupled with a thick, fluffy coat and a lengthy tail that stretches along their body, makes them appear even bigger. With large, tufted ears and oval-shaped eyes that glisten with discernment, this kitty has a reputation for intelligence, and with heaps of energy to match, it's a formidable companion.

Some believed the Maine Coon was the result of a wildcat breeding with a raccoon because of its super-puffy tail, but the truth is more straightforward. The original breed evolved from European cats, who were brought to the shores of New England in the US in the 17th and 18th centuries. These resilient moggies adapted to the harsh winters by developing a thick, water-resistant coat, large, snow-shoe shaped paws and a hardy constitution. Water babies at heart, Maine Coons love a bath and any excuse for a splash about.

CAT SUPERSTITION

BLACK CATS

Throughout history, black cats have received a bad press, but in truth, superstitions vary depending on which part of the world you're from. In Europe, during the early part of the 13th century, they were associated with witches and considered an ill omen. Their ability to navigate the darkness and move unseen made them seem supernatural, so people believed they were in cahoots with the Devil. In medieval times, it was commonly thought that any animal possessing dark fur or feathers was a portent of doom, and cats being nocturnal only added to this falsehood. The ancient Egyptians had a different view. To them, black cats resembled their beloved goddess Bastet, and this meant they were particularly auspicious and favoured. In medieval Japan, a black cat crossing your path was a sign you would find true love, while in Scotland, if one appeared on your doorstep, prosperity would soon follow.

THE CAT'S WHISKERS

LAPPING IT UP

A cat's tongue is a multi-faceted tool, being both a weapon and a brush in one. Equipped with hundreds of minute, backwards-facing spines known as papillae, which give the tongue a sharp scratchy feel against the skin, the tongue has the ability to strip meat from the bones and glean every last bit of nutrition. This would have been extremely useful to wild kitties, who needed to make the most of each morsel of prey. The tongue is also an efficient grooming tool, which not only cleans and detangles fur, but also redistributes saliva amongst the hairs. The papillae, which are scoop shaped, store the cleansing fluid within the tongue, ready to be smoothed upon the skin.

FELINE MYTH

THE YULE CAT

Also known as Jólakötturinn, this ferocious feline appears in Icelandic folklore as a reminder to be good and work hard. An enormous shadowy creature with fang-like teeth and glaring eyes, it emerges on Christmas Eve to stalk the wintry countryside and the local towns for prey. Those crossing its path should be sure to wear their best outfit, for this kitty has a discerning eye, and is on the lookout for those who did not receive new clothes for Christmas.

If you were one of the lucky ones, and had been bestowed with wealth or had worked hard during the year and received garments as a gift from your employer, then you were safe. Those who were poor or who had shirked their responsibilities were likely to become the Yule Cat's next meal. Terrified children would be told to hide beneath their bedclothes and behave so that they didn't attract the attention of the prowling feline. A popular legend retold at Christmastime, this folk tale was used as an incentive for industry and good behaviour for children and adults throughout Scandinavia.

FELINE SNUGGLE TIME

While toys and games are a great way to show your cat you care, the most important thing you can do to enhance their life is to be there for them. Cats have a reputation for being independent, but they also require lots of attention to be truly content. During the festive season things pick up pace in the human world, and there will be many demands on your time, but ensure you make space for your kitty too. Simple things such as having regular cuddle time and talking to your cat can soothe them and strengthen the bond between you. Go to them on their terms and sit together in their favourite spot. You don't have to do much except be there and share a quiet moment. It will do you both good to take some time out together.

THE ROCKING CROUCH

Cats crouch, flex and stretch as part of their daily routine, working their lower legs and extending their paws. This move helps to strengthen your legs and arms, and improve flexibility through the hips.

- Stand with your feet hip-width apart and your shoulders relaxed.

- Lengthen your spine and tighten your tummy.

- Take a deep breath in and raise your arms and hands above your head.

- Exhale, drop down into a squat, and let your arms gradually lower until your palms are flat on the floor and your arms are straight out in front of you.

- Inhale and rock forwards, placing more weight onto your hands, and pushing your thighs outwards with your elbows.

- Hold this position for a few seconds, then exhale and rock back, slowly rising to your feet.

CAT CHAT

BOXING CLEVER

Cats express themselves through actions. The things they do might seem odd to us, but there is always a reason for their quirky behaviour. Cardboard boxes, whatever the shape or size, are a source of fascination for felines. This is because the box provides comfort. It's an enclosed space where they can feel safe and view the world. It appeals to their predatory instincts too, as it gives them a vantage point from which to pounce upon their prey, be it an errant sock, your toes or their favourite catnip mouse. Couple this with the fact that it's super toasty and insulated, and you have the ideal sanctuary for your kitty and an inexpensive toy. Keep this in mind at this time of year, when you might be ordering lots of goodies online, and save the boxes. Just be sure to remove staples or any sticky packaging that can get stuck to fur and paws.

CAT SPELL

SPELL FOR A JOY-FILLED YEAR

While you can never fully predict the future, there's no better time of year to look ahead and think positively. Treat your cat this festive season and ensure that the following twelve months are filled with love, laughter and lots of foodie treats.

You will need: a small charm bag, a bell from an old collar, a sprig of catnip, lavender essential oil, a pinch of salt

Perform this spell any time during December in the lead-up to New Year's Eve. Pick a night when you can see the moon in the sky and stand by a window so that you can feel its light.

· Take the charm bag in both hands and say, 'From this moment on, and the twelve months to come, my cat will be happy, its days filled with fun. Each hour will be joyful, and love will be rife, may my feline be blessed with a happy life.'

· Add the bell and the catnip into the bag to promote play, then add two drops of the lavender essential oil for harmony.

· Add a pinch of salt for protection.

· Hang the sealed bag somewhere near your cat's favourite sleeping spot, but make sure it's out of their reach to avoid any accidents.

GLOSSARY OF MYSTICAL TERMS

ANCIENTS
People who lived thousands of years ago, who practised customs and traditions that tied into their beliefs

AURA
The energy field that surrounds the body

CANDLE MAGIC
A spell that uses a candle, or candles, to manifest a particular outcome

CHANT
A set of words, sometimes rhyming, that are repeated with magical intent as part of a spell or ritual

CHARM
An object imbued with specific magical energy, like a lucky coin, stone or crystal

CLEANSING
The spiritual practice of clearing negative energy from a space or the body's aura

DEITY
A supernatural being, also known as a god or goddess, that is considered divine or sacred

FOLKLORE
Stories, beliefs and customs, which are adopted by a culture and passed down through the generations

INFUSION
A tea made by steeping herbs and other ingredients in hot water to extract the oils and flavours

MANTRA
An inspiring statement that is often repeated

MEDICINE
The healing power associated with an animal, herb
or flower

MEDITATION
A mental exercise that uses focus and awareness, along with
relaxation, to clear the mind

MOON PHASE
The term used to describe the changing shape of the moon
in the sky

OMEN
A sign, either good or bad, which foretells the future

OTHERWORLD
A spiritual realm that exists alongside our own. Often used
to describe the fairy realm

RITE
A religious or sacred ceremony or act to mark an event

RITUAL
A series of magical actions performed in a set sequence, this
can include gestures, words and actions, and the use
of specific ingredients

SIXTH SENSE
A psychic sense, also called intuition, that relies on gut
feelings and instincts

SPELL
A wish to bring about change that combines intention with
energy, and sometimes uses external ingredients and words

SUPERSTITION
A belief or practice based on supernatural forces

SYMBOL
A sign, mark or shape that has particular meaning or is
associated with an idea or belief

TALISMAN
An object that is believed to have magical properties or
powers to avert evil and bring good luck

THIRD EYE
The psychic energy centre, or chakra, situated in the middle
of the forehead above the eyes

VISUALIZATION
The ability to see and picture what you would like to manifest
in your mind

WANING
The term used to describe the moon phase as it is getting
smaller in the sky

WAXING
The term used to describe the moon phase as it is getting
bigger in the sky

CAT GLOSSARY

CATNIP
A herb in the mint family which causes behavioural change in cats, often used for relaxation or fun

CAT CHAT
The purrs, miaows, chatters and chirrups made by your cat, which all have a difference purpose, sound and frequency

CAT STRETCH
The many poses a cat can strike, thanks to the unique biology of these animals

FUR COAT
Cats can be shorthaired, semi-longhaired or longhaired. The longer the fur, the more grooming a cat will require

MANEKI NEKO
The lucky cat or beckoning cat, with one paw raised; an auspicious symbol according to Japanese tradition

MAKING BISCUITS
The act of treading with the front paws, also known as 'kneading' – which looks like making biscuits

NICTATING MEMBRANE
The extra eyelid cats have, which is usually hidden

PAPILLAE
The spines on a cat's tongue, which make it feel rough and spiky

ABOUT THE AUTHOR

A professional storyteller with a keen interest in mythology, spirituality and the natural world, Alison Davies is the author of more than thirty books, including *The Mystical Year*, *The Self-Care Year* and *The Lunar Year*. She also runs writing workshops at universities across the United Kingdom.

ACKNOWLEDGEMENTS

I've been so lucky again to work with the brilliant, and ever-patient editor Sofie Shearman, and a heartfelt thanks goes to Alicia House for the gorgeous design. To the rest of the team at Quadrille – a huge thank you goes out to all of you for helping to create this special book.

I would also like to thank my copy editor Chloe Murphy, who once again used her enduring 'book magic' to make sense of the words on the page and sprinkle them with a little extra enchantment.

A huge thank you also goes out to the amazingly talented Anastasia for her wonderful illustrations, which capture the magical essence of all things feline, and bring my words to life. You are an artistic genius!

Cats are my world and so writing this book has been the *purr*fect project, a true joy, and definitely the cat's whiskers!

MANAGING DIRECTOR
Sarah Lavelle

PROJECT EDITOR
Sofie Shearman

SERIES DESIGNER
Emily Lapworth

DESIGNER
Alicia House

ILLUSTRATOR
Anastasia Stefurak

HEAD OF PRODUCTION
Stephen Lang

PRODUCTION CONTROLLER
Martina Georgieva

Published in 2024 by Quadrille Publishing Ltd

Quadrille
52–54 Southwark Street
London SE1 1UN
quadrille.com

The publisher has made every effort to trace the copyright holders.
We apologize in advance for any unintentional omissions and would
be pleased to insert the appropriate acknowledgement in any
subsequent edition.

Cataloguing in Publication Data: a catalogue record for this book
is available from the British Library.

ISBN 978 1 83783 137 1

Printed in China